Strength
for the
Journey

A GUIDE TO SPIRITUAL PRACTICE

Strength
for the
Journey

A GUIDE TO SPIRITUAL PRACTICE

Renée Miller

Photography by Diane Walker

With love & blessings to
Juanita. May these small
practices bring you into the
heart of God...

Renée Miller+

Morehouse Publishing
NEW YORK · HARRISBURG · DENVER

Isaiah 65:24

Unless otherwise noted, the Scripture quotations contained herein are from the New Revised Standard Version Bible, copyright © 1989 by the Division of Christian Education of the National Council of Churches of Christ in the U.S.A. Used by permission. All rights reserved.

Morehouse Publishing, 4775 Linglestown Road, Harrisburg, PA 17112

Morehouse Publishing, 445 Fifth Avenue, New York, NY 10016

Morehouse Publishing is an imprint of Church Publishing Incorporated.
www.churchpublishing.org

Cover art courtesy of Diane Walker

Cover design by Laurie Klein Westhafer

Library of Congress Cataloging-in-Publication Data
Miller, Renée, 1953–
 Strength for the journey : a guide to spiritual practice / Renée Miller.
    p. cm.
  ISBN 978-0-8192-2746-1 (pbk.)
  1. Spiritual life. 2. Christian life. I. Title.
  BV4501.3.M5475 2011
  248—dc22
                    2010054074

Printed in the United States of America

CONTENTS

FOREWORD

Strength for the Journey: A Guide to Spiritual Practice was published in 2011 as a journal of twenty reflections on finding the spiritual dimensions in the common activities that fill our days and nights.

CREDO Institute, Inc., an agency in the Episcopal Church that promotes and nurtures health and wellness for Episcopal Church Pension Plan participants, sought to publish this collection because living more healthy lives in the state of holistic wellness is a goal within the reach of everyone.

CREDO uses the handbook as a resource for conference participants who are exploring the boundaries and bridges of their spiritual lives. The book is more than a companion piece to the CREDO conference curriculum, however. In style as well as substance, *Strength for the Journey: A Guide to Spiritual Practice* reflects the essential approach behind CREDO and the impact it has on participants. At the core, CREDO is less about composing something novel and more about unveiling a narrative that was imagined long before.

CREDO espouses a process of self-efficacy and transformation familiar to CREDO conference participants as the IDPT cycle. This is a manner of self-discovery—or perhaps better understood, self-disclosure. By examining Identity, Discernment, Practice, and Transformation, we are not so much stumbling upon new things as rediscovering what has always been at the core of who we are and who God is calling our unique selves to be.

In the IDPT process, our Identity is as fixed and yet as fluid as an ocean and her tides. Our Discernment is less decision, more an opening to listen with our heart. Our Practice isn't to learn a new tune, but hear the echo of our heart's song through the valleys and canyons of our lives. Our Transformation completes the circle of change, and with Divine grace delivers us to a deeper sense of our renewed Identity.

Miller applies this idea to each reflection she uplifts. In examining the simple activities of everyday life, she helps the reader discover what is already there: God's simple presence.

In his insightful introduction, Brian Taylor draws from the experience of a Trappist monk at Spencer Abbey. "Monastic life is just putting a frame around everyday life. We do the same things everyone else does—we eat, we work, we sleep, we live in community. But we do it all with intention towards God, and that makes it holy."

Photographer, writer, and Episcopal communicator Diane Walker graces this project with her own eye for the sacred in everyday life. As a visual accompaniment to each reflection, the color photographs from Walker's camera draw us into deeper relationship with the world about us.

Herb Gunn
Director of Communication CREDO Institute Inc.

ACKNOWLEDGMENTS

No work of importance, it seems, is ever done alone. We were created to collaborate so that what thread each of us brings can become a completed tapestry of which we are all a part. This book really began many years ago in an office in Memphis, Tennessee, with three people putting their heads together to think of ways to deepen the spiritual component of the CREDO conference. The words I have written are merely an enfleshment of those shared ideas. I want to thank Bill Craddock and Gay Jennings for their creativity and deep, deep care of the clergy. I want to thank the entire CREDO community for the thoughts, stories, and questions that led to this book. I want to thank Herb Gunn for valuing communication enough to work hard to make sure that it happens. I offer gratitude for the soul and example of Brian Taylor, whose Introduction gives this book context and form. And finally, I thank Joan Castagnone, the editor of this work. Without her expert wordsmithing, this book would be deficient. With her uncanny ability to see inside my head and heart, she has given this book spirit.

—Renée Miller

INTRODUCTION

Brian C. Taylor

This guide to spiritual practice offers a diverse and extensive view of spiritual discipline. But before diving in, perhaps it might be helpful to remember why we practice disciplines in the first place. After all, we can undertake religious activities for all sorts of reasons: to satisfy an inner critic who says, "You're not spiritual enough"; to pursue emotional highs; or just to feel less stress. What is the context for spiritual discipline within the Christian life of faith?

Let's begin with the word "spirituality." Locate this category on the shelves in any major bookstore and you'll find hundreds of titles: from Buddhist meditation, to the spirituality of business, baking, and baseball, and everything in between—it's all out there. But what do we mean by this word?

For some, "spirituality" is the doing of spiritual practice such as those suggested in this guide: prayer and meditation, worship, study, ministry, movement. But there's a problem with this. When we don't practice, we believe that we're not being very spiritual. Even worse, when we do practice, we believe that we are! We all know pious, disciplined people who we wouldn't call "spiritual" at all. Jesus certainly came across some of those folk.

For others, "spirituality" means certain kinds of inner experiences, often characterized as calm, spacious, alert, loving, and serene, filled with a sense of connection with everything and everyone. As

1

accurately as these words might describe some of our experience, they are really the fruit of a spiritual life, not the thing itself. When calmness or a sense of connection becomes our definition of spirituality, we run the risk of making these experiences into idols. We seek these experiences rather than seeking God. When we don't feel these things, we assume that we are not "spiritual" or that God is absent.

So if spirituality is not *practice*, and it is not the hoped-for *fruit*, what is it?

It is *relationship*. Spirituality is how we are in relationship to God, to other people, to the world around us, and to ourselves. Spirituality is the process of staying engaged in these relationships, the intention we bring to them, and how willing we are to evolve as the relationship affects us.

Our relationship with God

Our tradition claims that while God is ultimately a mystery and beyond all of our definitions, God is also personal. While God cannot be reduced to a person (like us, only perfect and much bigger!), God is in relationship with us personally. The Creator of heaven and earth, the Spirit of all wisdom and harmony, the connective force of renewing life in the universe—this One hears our prayers, counts the hairs on our heads, and responds to the particularities of our situations.

We say that God loves us, and that we are called to love God with all our hearts, souls, minds, and strength. In this relationship, we pray, we struggle with our demons, we do our best to trust, and we give thanks. As in any intimate affinity, we are comforted, encouraged, challenged, exposed, forgiven, gifted, and empowered.

And as in every other relationship, we cannot control the outcome of our relationship with God. We may like to think that we know where this relationship will take us—into greater peace of mind, more patience, kindness and wisdom. In fact, these qualities are promised in scripture, in the lives of the saints, and to everyone who loves God. But along the way, our relationship with God may take us through some landscape that's not so pretty. We may need to get a lot angrier before we can find peace. We may need to move through a dark night of despair before we get to the light of God.

We are in relationship to the living God, who has a character, will, and methods that are not our own. Spirituality is our ongoing, evolving relationship with this living God. This is why it is so important to not confuse spiritual *fruits* or *disciplines* with spirituality itself, making an expected emotional state or the fulfillment of religious activity into something more than they are.

For Christians, Jesus is central to our relationship with God. He may be to us a friend, an enigmatic presence, or the very face of God. Our relationship to Jesus may change over time, just as our other relationships in life change.

And it is a relationship that Jesus always asks, nothing more. Sometimes I talk to seekers who are worried that they aren't "real" Christians because they don't hold to particular beliefs strongly enough. They think that unless they can resolve the place of Christ in the Trinity or the paradox of his full humanity and divinity, they can't genuinely claim to be a Christian.

My response is to ask them to read quickly through the synoptic gospels, asking themselves what Jesus expected of his disciples.

Usually what these seekers discover is that Jesus said, "Follow me. Come and see." He didn't demand moral perfection or theological certainty. He wanted people to be in relationship with him. In relationship, they would hear him, watch him in action, be questioned by him, and come to know his love for them. We might be in relationship with Jesus mystically, intellectually, sacramentally, or companionably. What matters is that as Christians, we somehow stay in an evolving relationship to Jesus Christ. He will affect us over time.

Our relationships with other people

How do we treat the waiter at the restaurant or the person checking out our groceries? How do we respond when the man at coffee hour makes a comment that opens to us, by just a crack, the door of his suffering? How do we tell people how much they mean to us? What kind of feelings do we cultivate towards people who are unkind or unfair to us? How do we exercise our gifts in the local church or in our social communities? And what kind of relationship do we have with people who don't share the privileges we enjoy?

When we bring our faith, our prayers, our questions, our scriptures, and our sacraments into these relationships, they are changed. The answers to the questions above will change as we see them in light of the gospel. Our behavior in these relationships will change as we pray, as we offer them in the Eucharist, as we puzzle over them with God. The application of our faith traditions to our relationships with others is what makes them "spiritual." It is also how we participate in the incarnation. For when we take our faith seriously enough to apply it directly to all of our relationships, God takes on human flesh.

Our relationship with the rest of creation

Spirituality is how we honor the earth and treat it with loving devotion, as God's own precious handiwork. It is how we stop and wonder at the color of the sky, the force of wind, the miracle of the flight of birds. It is how we live our daily lives as consumers of the earth's resources. Creation is God's body, and our spirituality is, in part, our intentional relationship with this magnificent, fragile, interconnected body.

Our relationship with ourselves

With just a bit of reflection, this notion can seem very strange: How can "I" be in relationship with "myself?" Aren't I one, not two? And yet we frequently say things like "I feel good about myself. . . . I've not really been myself lately. . . . I feel the need to change myself. . . . I'm learning to accept myself. . . . I really saw myself yesterday." An important question arises—*who is the subject* of the feeling good, changing, accepting, or seeing, and *who is the object*?

Without stepping too far into a metaphysical swamp in this brief introduction, suffice it to say that we humans are gifted with the unique capacity for self-reflection, for self-awareness. Different traditions explain this in different ways. Through the contemplative stream of our Christian tradition, we can understand it as the Spirit within us relating to our conditioned selves

We are born with genetic determinates and predispositions. As we develop, we are influenced by our circumstances and the people that surround us. We adopt responsive strategies that help us survive and progress. Along the way, some of these conditioned habits of mind, emotion, and behavior become helpful, and some become harmful. Some are our virtues, some are our sins. This is the conditioned self.

Meanwhile, we are also created in the image of God. Each of us is like a seed that contains great potential to fully become the person God intends us to become. The Spirit is given to help us evolve. As spiritual beings, we activate and affirm this Spirit through the sacraments, faith, devotion, and spiritual practice. Living through us, the Spirit becomes more and more part of our consciousness.

This makes it possible, at times, to see our conditioned selves with God's eyes. As Meister Eckhart said in a sermon, "The eye with which we see ourselves is the same eye with which God sees us." So it is "the Spirit bearing witness with our spirit" (Romans 8:16). And we can boldly say that as Christians—along with our sinful and limited humanity—"We have the mind of Christ" (1 Corinthians 2:16).

In the course of our faith journeys, the Spirit, the Christ within us, the image of God given to us in potential form—this true self rises up and relates to the conditioned self. Gradually, in the dance between God's grace and our efforts, we evolve. We "work out [our] own salvation with fear and trembling" (Philippians 2:12). Jesus and Paul go so far as to say that in the process, the [false] self dies, and "it is no longer I [the conditioned self] who lives, but Christ within me" (Galatians 2:20). And yet we remain uniquely ourselves, a particularly (in my case) "Brian-shaped" version of Christ, or image of God.

And so we say that we relate to ourselves. Our spirituality is how we live out this relationship with the self. Are we intentional about it? Are we lazy? Are we perfectionist? Do we believe it is all up to us? Are we waiting for God to zap us? Are we willing to go into the empty place of grace that remains when we walk away from conditioned habits of mind, emotion, and behavior? Can we live the tension between being determined to grow, forgiving ourselves for being human? Our spirituality, then, is how we are in relationship with God, other people, creation, and ourselves.

The place of spiritual discipline

With grace, with faithfulness, these relationships bear *fruit*. Our tradition tells us that over time, extending into eternity, all these relationships will be redeemed, that they will fulfill God's intentions: love, forgiveness and reconciliation; compassion, justice and peace; environmental harmony; and for you and me, that we will be filled with the light of God. All of this redemption is *the fruit* of our spirituality; it is the result of faithful relationships.

So what is our part in producing this fruit? Ah, this finally brings us to the subject and purpose of this guide: *practice*. Practices, or "spiritual disciplines," are the things we do intentionally that strengthen and enliven our relationship with God, others, the world, and the self. Spiritual practices are the things we do that, together with God's grace, produce the fruit of redemption.

Renée Miller has done a wonderful job of putting the spotlight on a variety of practices, some very traditional and some not so traditional. One gets the feeling that she could have kept going forever, highlighting hundreds more of them, because, after all, how we live in relationship to all of life is spiritual practice. We are to love God with all our hearts, minds, souls, and strength. In beginning to list spiritual practices, we end up like the author of John's gospel, when he spoke of the "other things" Jesus did, "If every one of them were written down, I suppose that the world itself could not contain the books that would be written" (John 21:25).

Perhaps spiritual discipline, therefore, is simply living in an awake, holistic, and faithful way. In a documentary film about the monastic life at Spencer Abbey, a Trappist monk said (and I paraphrase), "Monastic life is just putting a frame around everyday life. We do the same things everyone else does—we eat, we work, we sleep, we live in community. But we do it all with intention towards God, and that makes it holy."

Some of us are easily geared towards being disciplined. We exercise six days a week, we get up every morning and meditate and read for an hour, we always take our laundry to the cleaners every Friday afternoon. This was once my routine, and my wife called me "the human metronome."

During this period of my life, regular discipline was important; it was helpful. Like someone who practices scales and exercises on one musical instrument for many years in order to find the depths and beauty of music, the one who is spiritually disciplined might be more able to plumb the depths of their faith. Having searched this territory deeply, it will always then be near, always accessible.

But life changes us, and I'm not so disciplined anymore. My spiritual discipline is now more like what Brother Lawrence described as the "little interior glance." Others have always been this way, people who don't really need the regular discipline I needed. This little interior glance can be made while eating a meal, taking a walk, talking to a friend, sitting in a budget meeting, reading a book, surfing the Internet, or gazing at the clouds. This simplicity is what Renée illustrates as she leads us through her diverse examples.

A few last words of advice

Engage in practices that enliven you, not the ones you think you should do. As Dom John Chapman said, "Pray as you can, not as you can't." It's about nurturing relationship.

How or when redemption happens is a mystery. For "The kingdom of God is as if someone would scatter seed on the ground, and would sleep and rise night and day, and the seed would sprout and grow, he does not know how" (Mark 4:26–27).

Keep in mind what T.S. Eliot wrote: "For us it is just the trying. The rest is not our business" (East Coker, *The Four Quartets*).

Meditative Practice

Centering Prayer, Praying with Beads, Daily Office,
Discursive Meditation

Centering Prayer

Contemplative prayer is part of a reality that is bigger than itself.
It is part of the whole process of integration, which requires
opening to God at the level of the unconscious.

—Thomas Keating

We move at a pace in life that keeps our souls as busy as our bodies; our unconscious as full as our conscious minds. We are regularly challenged to switch between ideas, images, feelings, thoughts, and emotions with the speed of a computer alternating between programs. The effect on our souls is subtle and stealthy. Over time, we find it difficult simply to be still. We find it difficult to pray or believe that we are centered in the Divine Presence during prayer. When we are able to take the time to focus ourselves on communication with God, we find our minds assailed by those same ideas, images, feelings, thoughts, and emotions that plagued us before we sat down to pray. It seems that the moment we settle ourselves in God's presence, we find that we are thinking about a meeting we need to prepare for, or a soccer practice we need to shuttle our child to, or something we have forgotten to buy at the store, or the person in the hospital that needs a visit. We may force ourselves to complete the prayer period and wonder at the end of it if we've even prayed at all. Or, we may choose to truncate or postpone our prayer because we are frustrated by the constant chatter in our minds.

Centering Prayer, a contemporary version of the ancient practice of contemplative prayer, is not only a way to pray, but a way of prayer that has the potential to make a significant impact on the pattern of our lives when we are not praying. Thomas Keating, the Cistercian monk and master of Centering Prayer, says that we are not able to determine if the practice is making a difference in our souls based on what happens during the actual time spent in the practice. Rather, we know the prayer is effective in our lives by the comments we receive from others who begin to see a difference in us. When we simply sit faithfully in God's presence and stay there, even when thoughts distract us, we will find that we are able to bring the practice into the situations of our everyday lives. Instead of becoming focused on what may seem urgent but is ultimately unimportant, we find we are able to let it go, just as we have done during the course of the prayer practice itself. In other words, what we practice in the prayer is what we begin to live outside the time of prayer.

Centering prayer is a simple, though hardly easy, practice. After settling in the presence of God, we choose a sacred word as a symbol of our intent to remain in God's presence during the prayer period. As thoughts rise in us, we gently let them go and return to the sacred word. Thomas Keating uses a potent image. He says that as thoughts float across our consciousness, they are like boats on the surface of a river. When we are focused on what is on the surface of the river rather than the river itself we slip away from our original intention. The sacred word helps call us back to the place of stillness and faithful presence to God. It is the soft offering that affirms that we want to give our attention back to God. We continue the process of letting go of thoughts and returning to the sacred word throughout the time given to the practice—usually twenty to thirty minutes once or twice each day.

If you are contemplative and reflective you are probably easily attracted to this form of prayer. You may find that it provides respite from the rigors of daily demands. On the other hand, if you are active and highly verbal you might, at first, think centering prayer is unsuitable for your spiritual personality. After practicing it for some time, however, you may be surprised by the spiritual balance that you experience as a result of quieting yourself in the place of deep spiritual rest.

Praying with Beads

To pray is to listen to the One who calls you "my beloved daughter," "my beloved son," "my beloved child." To pray is to let that voice speak to the center of your being, to your guts, and let that voice resound in your whole being.

—Henri Nouwen

One of the most difficult aspects of prayer and meditation is focus. So much that occurs in the daily round of life distracts us during the time of prayer. If we were to count the number of thoughts we have in just one hour, we would be astonished at the capacity of our minds to flit like hummingbirds from thought to thought. In many ways, this is not a new phenomenon. We easily fault contemporary life and technology for what Buddhists call "monkey mind." Yet, it is more a primordial than a generational response. It is part of being human and it is a glorious part of being human. It is what makes dreaming, imagining, inventing, and creating possible. While we can quickly become discouraged during prayer with the plethora of stuff inside our minds moving us off focus, it is that very stuff that is responsible for our ongoing health and growth.

The real issue is in the timing. There are times when we want to be free of our bouncing thoughts in order to become inwardly still. There are times we want our focus to be as piercing as a laser beam. There are times we do not want any disturbance to interrupt our intention. An external aid can often help us find the peace and focus we seek. For centuries, in all religions, beads and prayer ropes have been such an aid. While the most familiar use of prayer beads is as a counter for the number of prayers said, its use extends far beyond its abacus function. Prayer beads are used to help channel the mind's energy to a single point with each bead representing a mantra or a prayer. As the user moves their fingers along the beads they are connecting mind and body in such a way that the soul is able to break free to be still in the presence of God. The fingering of the beads keeps the mind and body engaged so that the soul can enter the depths of divine love.

Episcopalians are most familiar with the Anglican Rosary that was developed in the 1980s as an aid for contemplative prayer. It is essentially a blend of the Roman Catholic Rosary and the Orthodox Prayer Rope. The Anglican rosary consists of twenty-eight beads with one Invitatory bead and four cruciform beads. The thirty-three beads are prayed three times, and a prayer is said with the cross so that the total number reaches one hundred. This is the same number used for the Orthodox Prayer Rope. Anglicans also use the Roman Catholic Rosary with slight adaptations. Islam, Buddhism, Hinduism, Sikhism, and Christianity all have some form of prayer beads. There is even an application for prayer beads for use on some mobile phones.

When we begin using beads as a prayer practice, we will need a certain amount of time to become so familiar with the practice and the prayers that they are repeated by memory rather than by conscious thought. Here, the intent is to "push the play button," so that the prayers will keep the mind occupied but not really thinking. This creates the space for the soul to descend more deeply into stillness. While we are learning the practice, we will not find ourselves descending as deeply as we will once the beads and their associated prayers have become one with our minds and the beating of our hearts. When that begins to occur, we will experience the kind of meditation that leads the soul into deep rest, into the divine embrace, into that space of holiness from which no one emerges unchanged.

If you feel a desire for contemplative prayer, but find it hard to sit still or keep thoughts at bay, you will find praying with beads a helpful way to go more deeply into your contemplative practice. If you are active by nature and would rather swallow ice whole than engage in contemplative prayer, you will find praying with beads a way to engage your active nature. The infinite variations available for praying with beads will appeal to anyone who is easily bored by repetition. As a reminder to pray, as a counter of prayer, as an aid for stillness, as a way to stay physically and mentally active, as a path for staying spiritually engaged, prayer beads can become one of our soul's treasured possessions.

The Daily Office

Seven times a day I praise you.
—Psalm 119:164a

It's so easy to get distracted. We set our minds to working on a task, set up a structure and timeline to complete it, and then find ourselves missing the deadline because something else comes along that needs our more immediate attention. We might plan to wash the car on Saturday, for example. Then, by the time Saturday rolls around, we forget about the car because our child has to go to soccer practice, our spouse has a function we must attend, or something from the office requires our attention. It's not that washing the car isn't important, but it seems less important than the other things that feel so insistent.

Our relationship with heaven can be easily forgotten in the events of a day. There is so much to do, so many conversations to have, so many errands to run, so many tasks to complete. Our shy and unassuming soul waits patiently for us to see its desire for connecting with the Holy One. But the distractions keep us from noticing that inner longing.

The Hebrew practice from the Psalms of praying seven times a day is not meant to be an onerous and impossible commandment.

It is meant to be the soft nudge that will help us stay tethered to what is most important in our lives—union with the Divine. If we develop the pattern and practice of turning our souls to God throughout the day, we will find that our souls stay full and our hearts remain still. The ancient spiritual pattern of praying the Offices is a way of centering the soul in the presence of God throughout the day.

We often think of saying the Offices either as an outdated and uninteresting form of prayer, or as a liturgical practice that is more communal than meditative. In truth, the Offices are infinitely flexible, and many creative variations can be used while retaining the structure that, for centuries, has kept souls close to heaven.

The word "Office" comes from the Latin word *opus* meaning work. Praying the Offices, like other spiritual practices, can sometimes seem like work we would rather not do. This prayer practice, however, has the capacity to draw us into something that makes more of our souls, more of our lives, more of the world. Like a musical opus by Mozart or Beethoven, it is a work of spiritual magnitude that can easily be missed simply because we are looking for something more exciting and trendy. Yet, if we embrace the humble and repetitive, sometimes boring, daily-ness of it, we will be astonished by the enormity of its power.

Unlike some other spiritual practices, praying the Offices is both an active and a contemplative experience. It draws upon the discursive part of our beings as well as the reflective. In it we taste the textured word of God in scripture, we pray the prayers of intercession and petition, we confess the times we've missed the mark and caused separation, we acknowledge and re-commit to the faith that is in us, we get down and dirty with the daily rigors and stresses of life as we work our way through the Psalms, and we have ample time to allow the finger of heaven to etch words on our souls in silence.

There are three strategies that will help us to receive the fullest spiritual benefit from this ancient practice. First, we need to give ourselves the freedom to adapt the Offices to what is important in our own prayer styles. This makes it a more relevant practice for modern life. For example, we can substitute other Collects or write our own, we can play a favorite piece of music for a canticle, or we can do five minutes of yoga or centering prayer as a response to one of the readings. What is most important, however, is to stay with whatever pattern we choose until it becomes second nature to us. The most grace-filled element of praying the Offices is that they become a kind of mantra for deep meditation. In other words, when we have them memorized, or practically so, we stop sitting on the edge of the pool with our feet dangling in the shallow end. Instead, we jump into the deep end and find ourselves enveloped in the full water of God's embrace. If we continually change the pattern every day, we remain at the edge of the pool.

Second, we need to make a commitment to consistency. This will keep our souls regularly poised for heaven's whisper and touch. Like any other practice in life, it is the consistency of the practice that yields the results. Over time, the commitment to consistency will lead us to a place of deep desire—desire that is more profound than the simple eagerness to try something new, or experience the good feeling of having done what we thought we should do. The deeper desire is to find the Holy One when our souls are empty and dry, to be held in the rugged embrace of heaven, to taste and chew the words of God that are sometimes bitter, sometimes sweet.

Perhaps, the Offices have remained such a powerful spiritual tool, precisely because they have been prayed consistently throughout the centuries. They are still prayed daily all over the globe; God's blessing has been called down into people's hearts and onto the world day after day for hundreds of years.

Third, we need to trust that even if our hearts don't feel the value of the prayer, God is there waiting to tend our languishing hearts. We need to trust enough that we are willing to wrap our hearts around the practice so tightly that it becomes natural to us even on days when words seem useless and prayers feel empty. We need to trust that when the practice is threaded into our souls like strands of wool, they will become solid and strong. We need to trust that the buffeting of the stresses and struggles of life will not interrupt or interfere with the tightly woven relationship between us and God. When we trust this much, we are more able to detach from difficulty and re-attach to ardor.

Praying the Offices is an attractive form of prayer if you find communal and liturgical prayer nourishing. It may be more difficult for you if you are tired of praying in a formulaic manner or if you feel it is a practice that is irrelevant to contemporary life, or if you prefer to simply rest in God rather than manage lectionaries, books, and Bibles. The Office, however, is an ancient prayer practice that offers more than words can express. You must try and try again until it becomes part of your day, until the day is not complete without it.

Discursive Meditation

We should not fix our desires on health or sickness,
wealth or poverty, success or failure, a long life or short one.
For everything has the potential of calling forth in us
a deeper response to our life in God.
Our only desire and our one choice should be this:
I want and I choose what better
leads to the deepening of God's life in me.
—St. Ignatius, The Spiritual Exercises

A disciple once asked one of the desert fathers how she could know that her prayer was making a difference. "I sit in my cell in solitude and silence, but I hear nothing. When will my prayer reach heaven?"

"Do not expect that because you sit in silence, heaven will come down. Instead, chew on the words of heaven until your tongue speaks to God as you are speaking to me. Heaven will see your effort and grant you grace." The desert father was trying to explain that meditation is more than simply sitting still and waiting. It is also about thinking and reflecting. The labor of this is not lost on heaven. When God sees the seriousness we bring to the task, and hears us trying to converse, God will respond.

The word discursive comes from the word discourse and refers to having a conversation. When we think of meditation, conversation is not usually what we think about. We move quickly to being silent and still, waiting on God to communicate with us in some way. It seems that prayer is comprised of conversation, while meditation is comprised of contemplation. In fact, meditation can include both conversation and contemplation.

Discursive meditation involves digging, speaking, and listening. When we engage in discursive meditation we gnaw on a scriptural principle or spiritual truth like a dog with a meaty bone. We look at it from different angles, consider how it might be practiced in different situations, attempt to penetrate its nuances in order to develop new patterns of behavior that will bring us closer into the embrace of heaven. To begin, choose a scripture passage or story for the time of meditation and offer a short prayer of intention. Read the passage and reflect on it in a logical and systematic way by asking questions such as these: Who is involved here? What is actually happening? What has created the circumstances in this passage? Why do people respond as they do? What other responses are possible? How do I experience God? When do I miss the presence of God or turn from it? Where do I fit in? How can I respond to this in my own life?

The deep interior and honest reflection that we give these questions helps us grow in understanding of spiritual principles and mature in faith. When the meditation period has ended, we carry our intentions with us into daily life where prayer is actually lived.

Three elements of discursive meditation are particularly helpful in creating these new contours in our souls. First, discursive meditation engages the mind, which teasingly becomes over-active the moment we try to settle into contemplative prayer. Second, it takes us into the holy stories in a way that makes them and us real. Finally, it leads to a makeover of our souls and a behavior change in our bodies. We are no longer so willing to stand on the outside watching to see how we will be re-shaped by people and situations in our lives. Instead, we become the active participants in the drama of life, praying that we will grow more and more into the likeness of God in all circumstances and with all people in our lives.

Lest we think that discursive meditation is too heady, too logical, too left-brained, we will find that all forms of discursive meditation offer some aspect of contemplation. We use the mind to sift and sort, study and sense, but at any point in the prayer when we feel a particular affective longing rising in us for the Divine One, we simply drop down into stillness and contemplation. There, in the moments of sublime silence we find our souls filling up and filling out, and we are gladdened with the spiritual power we experience when we simply take the time to come apart and rest awhile.

Two familiar forms of discursive meditation are *Lectio Divina* and Ignatian Prayer. **Lectio Divina**, the pattern established by St. Benedict in the fourth century, combines elements of both discursive and contemplative prayer. The four movements of *lectio divina* include: reading, meditation, prayer, and contemplation. We begin by taking a passage of scripture and reading it slowly and deliberately—as if savoring a plate of the finest and most exquisite food. This opens the door to deep reflection and meditation. This is the point at which questions are asked, possibilities are turned over in the mind, new patterns of insight are sought, and applications of the biblical story are applied to our personal human stories.

As we enter into the passage and see the intersection between ourselves and God, we easily move into a time of discourse or conversation with God. Our spirits are moved by what we have thought and considered, what we have tasted and twirled in our mouths like fine wine, and the result is a yearning to be in an encounter of prayer with the One who is at once beyond us and as close to us as the steady beating of our hearts. When all our words have been expended, and our thoughts have been emptied into the heart of heaven, we are ready to simply rest in God. We are ready to be still. We are ready to let our minds cease activity and come to a point of absolute quiet. In the soft movement of our breath, and the peacefulness of our minds, we find the hand of God massaging our souls into something new. We make a commitment to a small step of action and feel ready to go forward with gratitude for the time we have spent with God.

Ignatian Prayer is based on the Ignatian Exercises developed by Ignatius of Loyola in the early 1500s to help retreatants identify God's will and follow through on it in their daily lives. Ignatian meditation uses the mind and the senses to better understand the biblical story and to enter more fully into it in order to change behavior. Through the process of prayer we begin to see our strengths and weaknesses, where our habits have become our prisons, and what we can do to better enflesh the life of Jesus in our own lives.

The meditation begins with a brief time of centering to acknowledge that we are in the presence of God. After we make an intention for the prayer time, we slowly work through the chosen scripture passage by mentally placing ourselves at the scene. We try to imagine all the details of the space/place as a preparation for applying all of our senses imaginatively to the scene. If a Gospel passage is selected, the connection between us and the life of Jesus is strengthened. As we enter the story, we encounter Christ and are led to ask ourselves and Jesus what needs to be attended to in our lives, what needs further reflection, what waits to open us to a new way of being. In this intimate encounter we find a desire to become more than we were before, to give ourselves more fully to the Creator and lover of our souls.

When we have imagined the scene, applied our senses to it, met Jesus in it, and identified ways in which we can carry it into our lives, we find ourselves in a discourse or conversation with Jesus that deepens intimacy and leads to personal growth and change. The meditation comes to a close with a prayer such as the Lord's Prayer. At any point in the reflection or at the end of the conversation, we may find our souls becoming still and our hearts longing only to sit with Jesus in silence and contemplation. The very work that engages the mind becomes the food for contemplative prayer.

If you find your soul longing more for sitting meditation than thinking meditation, you may find patterns of discursive meditation unsettling at first. After a few days, however, the hunger for reflection creates a longing to dig even more deeply into the stories that have the potential to re-work the outlines of your soul. On the other hand, if you are immediately drawn to this type of meditation because you appreciate the thoughtful, reflective, and logical style of it, you will be surprised when that very thinking and reflecting unexpectedly leads to simply being still and quiet.

Ministry Practice

Caring, Hospitality, Money, Gratitude

Caring

Caring about others, running the risk of feeling,
and leaving an impact on others, brings happiness.

—Harold Kushner

Innocence and freedom from responsibility seem to bring with them an element of unselfish caring. There's no negative history or over-activity to cloud our caring responses. After we have been battered and pummeled by life, however, or have become overly involved in what are considered to be the important things of life, simple caring becomes as slippery as an eel. It's not that we no longer care. It's that our caring too easily becomes confined. It is carried out mostly in the relationships that take up our lives with a few random acts of kindness sprinkled in.

We find ourselves caring for those in our families, those in our congregations, those in our workplaces, those in our circle of friends. There is precious little time left over for caring for people that are outside our everyday circles. We may, from time to time, find ourselves doing a specific ministry that is not a part of our normal routines, but for the most part, our caring is confined to our circle of relationships or our ministries.

The Old English word for caring—caru—means sorrow, grief, or anxiety. Although this is a surprising description of the word, it holds within it an aspect that is critical to the spiritual practice of caring. When we commit to the practice of caring, we become aware and attentive to the sorrow, grief, or anxiety that rises in us when we see others struggling and in need. It is, as Kushner says, "running the risk of feeling." When we truly risk feeling, we are no longer able to ignore, avoid, or deny the reality of people's needs. The spiritual practice of caring begins when we decide to risk feeling.

There are many ways to take on caring as a spiritual practice. The foundation of the practice lies in the attentiveness we give to the movement of deep feeling we experience. This sometimes requires intentional focus if we are so accustomed to caring in our work that we are not as aware of our feelings when they are triggered by a person or situation not connected with our ministries.

In order to develop this kind of focus and attention, we need to open ourselves to the needs of others on a regular basis. We can do this by committing ourselves to a ministry that has no connection whatever with what we do in our daily work. Or, we might align ourselves with a community project that cares for the underprivileged in the community. Or, we might push ourselves beyond our comfort zones to give care to a group of people that we find difficult to accept or love. Or, we might enter into a relationship with someone who experiences hardship on a daily basis. Or, we might even travel to care for those in a developing country. When we encounter what we don't understand, what we are fearful of, or what is unknown to us, and feel the sorrow and grief of compassion growing in us, we are ready for the practice of caring.

Such radical compassion causes three things to happen in our souls. First, we grow in gratitude. We become grateful for the lives and blessings that we have been given, but even more we become grateful for the recipients of our caring. Through them we begin to see the places in our souls that have lain empty for too long. We gain insight into how those empty places might be filled. Hope begins to trickle into us and our hearts begin to gladden.

Second, we are diverted from our own struggles. As we notice and respond to the grief and sorrow that creep up in our souls, when we relate with those in need, we find that we are no longer so absorbed in our own dramas and story lines. As we open ourselves to what is outside of and beyond us, we are less fascinated with the often trivial stresses that occupy our mind and souls.

Finally, the practice of caring helps us pull back the mantle on meaning. The purpose of human existence, the power of God, the strength of human community is revealed in ways that had before seemed obscure. The practice of caring takes us out of ourselves and into the heart of God through the hearts of others.

If you find social interaction natural and easy you will find the spiritual practice of caring a meaningful extension of your desire to be involved in giving hope and life to others. If you are more introverted, you may at first, turn away from a commitment to caring practice for fear that it will be too demanding, too consuming. When, however, compassion is manifested internally, it will long to be expressed outwardly. When inward compassion is given wings, we are awakened to a deeper sense of holy presence.

Hospitality

I saw a stranger yestreen:
I put food in the eating place
I put drink in the drinking place
I put music in the listening place;
and in the blessed name of the Triune
he blessed myself and my house;
And the lark said in her song
often, often, often
goes the Christ in the stranger's guise.
                    —An old Gaelic rune

The way to understand hospitality practice is to back into it. We often think of hospitality as little more than entertaining guests—family, friends, and sometimes, strangers. We put food in the eating place, drink in the drinking place, as a way of sharing hearth and home with others. Sometimes we're blessed and filled by our guests, and sometimes we just wish they would go home. Offering hospitality can be both energizing and draining, depending on our moods, the personality of the guests, and the degree of perfection we try to achieve in what we offer. At its foundation, we know that hospitality is simply welcoming others into our space and sharing the simple things of food and conversation with them. Yet, we can still make hospitality into a work of heroism to rival any fabulous dinner put on by the Queen of England. At the end of it, we're worn out and want to be left alone for a while. If this experience of hospitality sounds familiar to us, we may be hesitant to grasp on to hospitality practice as the best way to knit our souls into the heart of God.

So, it's best to understand hospitality by backing into it. Take a few moments to remember when hospitality has been extended to you. When have you felt truly welcomed? When have you felt truly included? When have you been so blessed by someone's hospitality that your own heart overflowed with gratitude?

We understand hospitality best by reflecting on the most profound moments of hospitality that have been offered to us. Most likely, the acts of hospitality that stand out in our memories are those that were simple and genuine. They may not have any connection whatsoever with food or drink or shelter. They may be simply moments when another person unexpectedly gathered us up into their circle of friendship, or accepted us as we were, or loved us in spite of ourselves. They may be encounters with people outside our ethnicity or social standing. They may be nothing more than a flight attendant noticing that we needed another bag of peanuts.

Henri Nouwen spoke about "hospitality of heart." At its core, hospitality is an opening of the heart. It really has very little to do with having friends or strangers over for dinner. Indeed, we can invite the poor into our homes for a meal three nights a week, but if our hearts are not open, we have not offered hospitality. This is what makes many of us avoid hospitality as a practice. We hesitate to open our hearts to the degree required by hospitality. Providing a meal or shelter seems more manageable than opening our hearts.

Opening our hearts means we really have to gather others in. Their problems, their dreams, the injustices done to them, the hopes that lie hidden in their souls, the joys that have taken them to heaven's doors—all these become a part of our own hearts when we engage in hospitality as a spiritual practice. The challenge of this, of course, is that the contents of our own hearts merge with those of our guest. This means that what is in our hearts is no longer front and center. It's no longer all about me. It becomes, instead, all about us. That internal shift can be difficult to make. It is particularly difficult when the ones we open our hearts to are completely unlike us. They may be of a different background, have a different educational level, enjoy different foods, have a career that seems strange to us, wear clothes that are offensive to us, have tattoos or body piercings that unsettle us, or speak, think, act, or feel in ways that are completely other than all that we find comfortable. It's much easier to have our favorite friends over for dinner and call it hospitality than it is to open our hearts to those who are different. It's even harder to then be asked to let the contents of their hearts merge with our own. Yet, this is exactly the invitation that hospitality practice offers us. The paradox, of course, is that when we have the courage to fully open our hearts to those we love, to those who are strangers, and to those who are as different from us as a coyote is from a dove, we find that, in the name of the Triune God, they bless us and our lives are never the same again.

Like other spiritual practices, hospitality practice needs to be done regularly and consistently. We may need to set a schedule in order to be faithful to our commitment to this practice, because it is so easy to avoid. In order to get the full benefit of hospitality practice, it is also important to step out in places where we've never been, to meet people we've not known before, to experience arenas of life beyond our familiar terrain. In this, hospitality practice is not only about gathering others in, but going where others are in order to open our hearts to them there.

If you are naturally extroverted, or enjoy conversing with and learning from others, you will find hospitality practice attractive. The struggle will not be so much the opening of the heart, but the closing of the mouth in order to hear the soft longings trying to be spoken from another's soul. If you are more interior and introverted, you may bristle at even the thought of engaging in this practice. The struggle will not be opening the heart or closing the mouth. It will be offering hospitality to those you don't know or those with whom you have no comfortable relationship. Like any practice that pushes us in new directions, whether it be jogging around a track, or hanging around an unfamiliar cafe in order to meet new people, the most important step is the first one. If we simply remember how we felt when someone opened their heart to us, it won't be so difficult to do it for someone else.

Money

Do not value money for any more nor any less than it's worth;
it is a good servant, but a bad master.

—Alexander Dumas

It is hard to calculate the importance of money in our lives—the amount of stress it gives us, the ignorance we sometimes feel about it, the untold good it has done in our own or others' lives. Most of us have, at one time or another had some conflict with money. During those times, we probably wished that we either had more of it, or that it would become less important in our lives and society. It is just paper and metal, yet it drives whole civilizations. Sometimes it feels like it has become our master rather than our servant.

Understanding money as a spiritual practice requires first an examination of our attitudes about it. If we are not intentional about this step of the process, we are likely to reduce money practice to nothing more than faithful stewardship. Stewardship is certainly a part of money practice, but if we think of it as only that, we will find that once we feel comfortable with our stewardship level, we will be tempted to stop there rather than dig deeper to understand how our relationship with money impacts our souls. If we reduce money practice to faithful stewardship, we may also miss out on the nuances of its blessing and miracle in life.

Doing the investigative, explorative, and soul-searching work about our money attitudes will carve a channel in our brains and in our souls that begs for the goodness of God to flow. Our money attitudes are often what keep that channel a mere vein rather than a pumping artery. In truth, money has no real power of its own. It's our attitudes that give it its power—both for evil and for good. Since many of our money attitudes have been formed from childhood, this part of the practice is even more important if we hope to find a way for money to strengthen our lives with God and others. Awareness, reflection, and action are the exercises that money practice asks of us. As we confront our own relationship with money, we may even find we are able to serve as models to others about the importance of this aspect of soul work.

In many ways, money practice is really a faith practice. It's not so much about dollars and cents, but about the way we incorporate trust in our lives. We all know the truth of this. When we are comfortable with our incomes, we may be more dependent on ourselves than God. Since we are doing the providing, our trust need not be so strong. But, if we lose a job or the revenue stream dries up, suddenly we become dependent on God rather than ourselves and our trust increases. If our attitudes about money are not examined alongside our patterns of trust, we will find ourselves living a seesaw life when it comes to our finances.

Money practice, then, asks us to examine how we feel about money, what decisions we make in our lives that are direct results of our money attitudes, how our faith in God's providence and care is linked to our beliefs about money, what causes us to avoid dealing with money, or what makes us greedy for more. Money practice begins with this examination because, until we are clear about issues such as these, our relationship with our money will remain distorted. We may find that we experience guilt when we have more than enough money, or we may find it difficult to part with the money we have. Money, as a medium of exchange, is just that—a medium of exchange. The potent question in this examination phase of money practice is, "What am I exchanging for money and why?" This involves not only goods and services, but also the work that we do. We need to assess what we are willing to shell out money to obtain, and what we are willing to do in order to gain it.

The second phase of money practice involves how we relate to the money we have. Again, our money attitudes will need to be considered. Do we avoid money because we think we're just not good with figures? Do we obsess over it because we are fearful we won't have enough? Do we feel anger because it doesn't seem adequate for the amount of work we do? Do we hoard it like Scrooge because we want protection and security? Do we risk it because we think there's always more where that came from? Do we give it away because we feel that it fulfills some religious expectation? Do we give it away with abandon and hilarity because "it's only money"? Do we trust that there will always be enough because God promised to look after us the way God looks after the birds and the flowers of the field? Do we feel it's up to us to work for it and manage it because God isn't all that concerned about it? Do we leave it up to others to deal with because we don't want the headaches and stress? All of us have developed patterns of behavior around our use of money. Money practice helps us uncover those patterns and determine whether or not they need to be revised.

Finally, money practice involves taking the physical and spiritual dimensions of money seriously enough in our own lives that we are able to model something of value for others. Everyone has a relationship with money, and that relationship is both material and immaterial. It is not only physical, it is also spiritual. For example, clergy are often unmotivated to spend much time with the money side of things. They would rather focus on personal or pastoral concerns. Yet, clergy as spiritual leaders, have the opportunity to help a vast number of people begin to make the connection between their money and their soul, but only if they have discovered the astonishing and life-giving connection themselves. Money practice helps us do just that.

If you are logical and enjoy working with numbers, you may quickly engage with the idea of money as a spiritual practice. But, because you enjoy figures, you may find it difficult to go deeply enough into your own soul to see where your faith and money meet. If you are intuitive and creative, you might want to have as little to do with money as possible, preferring to bury your head in the sand than be overwhelmed by the chaos you think swirls around money issues. For all of us, however, money practice is a way to calm the chaos, get clear about the role of money in our lives, and deepen the faith that we have in God with or without paper and metal.

Gratitude

Gratitude is when memory is stored in the heart and not in the mind.
—Lionel Hampton

In the regular run of a day, we often find ourselves consumed by events and encounters. We try to attend to what is right before us at the same time that we're thinking of the next situation ahead. Gratitude may flit across the canvas of our souls from time to time when we experience some unexpected moment of grace, but it does not usually flow like a steady mountain stream all through the day.

When we think of gratitude we naturally think of being thankful that something good has happened, or that we have witnessed something outside our normal experience that has left us feeling some measure of awe, or that something difficult has taken a turn for the better. We are not as ready to feel grateful in the midst of hardship and struggle, or when those we love suffer injustice or indignity, or when our dreams are dashed, or when our hope or faith is tried or lost. That's when gratitude seems an unlikely companion. We figure we'll feel gratitude when there's something to be grateful for—when things change and are back to the way we believe they should be.

In fact, it is possible to experience gratitude as a steady mountain stream running through our days, but only if we approach it as something that applies to all of life no matter whether the situations that surround us swirl like a tornado or whisper like a gentle balmy breeze. Gratitude is not really dependent on having something positive to respond to, but a way of life waiting to be expressed. When we focus gratitude only on one part of life—what we perceive to be the grace of life—we miss the subtler grace that is always present in darkness, in struggle, in difficulty. Gratitude shines a light on the darkness, the struggle, the difficulty and in the pockets of brightness, we notice the grace that seemed before to be hidden from view. Though we had not expected it, we find our souls filling with gratitude for that grace.

There are few spiritual practices as enjoyable and fulfilling as gratitude practice for two simple reasons. First, it lets us re-live blessing and grace and in this we have the experience twice. Just consider all the moments and experiences where the presence of God has been felt, the times when grace has hovered like a bank of coastal fog. Those memories are stored in our hearts and etched on our souls. Gratitude is the way we access them again and again. Gratitude practice invites us into the past where we experience those moments anew. Gratitude practice invites us into the present where grace peeks out like a wildflower in winter. Gratitude practice invites us into the future where we are expectant in the promise of grace yet to be revealed.

Second, gratitude builds on itself, and in this we find that even when we thought something had no redeeming value, grace still peers out like a shy child waiting to be coaxed out from hiding. Sometimes it's difficult to find that shy child in the midst of situations that damage our hearts, or leave us in darkness, or fling our joy out the window, or challenge every bit of faith we have. We are so consumed with seeing ourselves through calamity that most of our energy is directed toward "crisis management." We console ourselves with the belief that God is with us, but finding the good and the grace-filled in the midst of it all can feel impossible. Gratitude practice helps us go back and look more deeply for the grace that seemed so distant, but it also helps us develop the skill for spotting grace even in the most dire circumstances.

When we begin gratitude practice, it is good to determine the strength of our gratitude muscles. We can do that when, after using the Preparatory Prayer Process (see pages 132–134), we write down one hundred things for which we are grateful. At first we'll find that we write very quickly. Our mind seems to pop with things that make us feel gratitude. Before we are halfway done, however, we'll find ourselves going a little more slowly. The further we go, the deeper we need to dig. Toward the end of the list, we'll be looking for the smallest, most stealthy graces—and they will be there. When we finally complete the list, we will feel both a spiritual weariness and a spiritual rejuvenation. This exercise will be a jump start for regular and consistent gratitude practice. As we progress in the practice, we begin to find that, rather than being grateful in hindsight, our souls are on the lookout for ways to see grace and be grateful for it.

Gratitude practice is beneficial for every spiritual personality. It is both an internal practice and a practice of ministry. We find our own souls expanding every time we feel and express gratitude, and when we're grateful, we find that our lives expand as well. Those who are grateful bring grace into the lives of others. As stated before, gratitude builds on itself and when we grow in gratitude others grow in theirs. One moment of gratitude leads to another, and in the end, we have hearts filled with joy.

Media
Practice

Technology, Music, Art, Movies

Technology

Technology is a gift of God.
After the gift of life it is perhaps the greatest of God's gifts.
It is the mother of civilization, of arts, and of sciences.

—Freeman Dyson

So much of our work and lives have become dominated by the computer. Most of us find the possibilities of technology exciting. We are awed by the immediate connection we have with the global community. We appreciate the ability to access information that would have been impossible to find only a few years ago. We even find that the computer has increased communication and community. And we look toward unforeseen and incredible opportunities that the computer will afford us in the future. At the same time, we experience the limits of technology. We see the ways that the computer can swallow up whole hours and days of our lives while we are hardly aware of the fact. In this way, we feel it steals part of our lives away. We recognize that the speed at which we can gain information also makes it tempting for people to expect us to work as fast as the computer. Their immediate issue, they feel, should become ours. We wonder about the long-term effects of computer use on the quality of relationships. We are both entranced by technology and cautious.

When the use of the computer is linked to the nurture of our souls, we may find ourselves even more resistant than usual. How can the computer, which is so individually oriented, be helpful in deepening spirituality? "People need to be in community—seeing and being with each other one-on-one, to have a full experience of the soul," we hear ourselves saying. And for ourselves, we may use the computer for work, for learning, for connecting with family and friends, for entertainment, but can't imagine how or why we would use it as a spiritual practice.

Technology practice has the capacity to take us from disbelief, to wonder, to the heart of God. There are so many possible ways to use the computer for spiritual practice. There are worship services we can download to our iPods, guided meditations, Bible study, spiritual questions to ponder and journal about, prayer communities to join, and new forms of prayer to explore. There seems to be an endless array of opportunities to feed our souls.

Imagine coming in to your office in the morning after a harried commute. You are already stressed when you see the pile of messages, the tasks left undone, and your calendar that seems too full for any sane person. You turn your computer on with a touch of resignation, and a momentary desire to begin your day with a game of solitaire. Instead, you sit down in your chair, pull up a spiritual site such as *www.belief.net* or *www.explorefaith.org* and find a practice for meditation. You may soon find yourself praying with an icon or other piece of art. You find your mind calming, your heart slowing, your soul opening. You have forgotten what is on your desk or planned for your day. You feel yourself being drawn like an ant to honey into the place of God's loving presence. You pray for a few minutes with the art, then click to Praying the Hours. Your last few minutes of technology practice is spent praying in the pattern that has sustained souls for centuries. After a moment of recollection, your spirit feels nourished and you are ready to greet your day.

This scenario can occur several times in a day, and each time we find ourselves staring at the screen, we also find our souls settling into the presence of God. Technology practice provides us with three important gifts. First, its solitariness. There is something potent and powerful in the way that we relate to God individually. We are corporately the children of God, but we are first individual children of God. Our souls need to approach God in solitude where the relationship between child and divine parent can be nurtured. Solitude is difficult to carve out in the course of a busy day. Sometimes the most solitude we experience is when we are working at our computers. This is, in fact, one of the criticisms of computer use—it shuts others out. Spiritually, we can use this to our advantage. When we engage in technology practice, we are generally less interrupted during those few minutes than we might be if we were just reading Morning Prayer at our desks. The solitariness that we claim in technology practice makes us more effective, more centered, even more prayerful when we enter again into the community of other human beings.

The second gift technology practice gives us is breadth. We do not have to be limited by the standard spiritual practices that have become almost mundane to us. We have the whole spiritual world around us, we have practices of holiness from around the globe to assist us, we have the wisdom of the ages at our fingertips.

Technology practice gives us the opportunity to stretch ourselves beyond what we know in order to experience what we do not know. In that process, our souls are broadened and our growth in God is expanded.

The third gift of technology practice is community. It seems paradoxical that sitting alone in front of a computer could lead us more deeply into community, but that is exactly what happens. We are ushered into the community at prayer throughout the world, we are ushered into the innumerable cast of saints on the planet, we are ushered into the absolute truth that we are not alone in this life or the next.

If you are a techno-geek you will naturally find yourself excited about experimenting with technology practice. There the cutting-edge possibilities may offer you an unsuspicious openness to finding God through the computer. If your spiritual life has been structured around more traditional and formal practices you may find it befuddling to think of engaging in computer practice even when those same traditional and formal practices can be found on the computer. What is important to remember, however, whether you are a techno-geek or someone who distrusts the value of technology, is that God's presence is available to you in all places when you have the eyes to see and the ears to hear.

Music

Music and rhythm find their way into the secret places of the soul.
—Plato

We are a culture obsessed with words. They help us make sense of ourselves and our world. They make it possible to communicate and get things done. They are a way to petition the Creator of the universe. But they are certainly not the only way to engage heaven. One of the most subtle and sublime ways to be connected with what is beyond our physical and spiritual sight is to pay attention to the other language of the soul—music. There, in the notes and tones, the rhythms and beats, the modulation and cadence, we find ourselves taken to that interior place where God dwells, where heart and heaven meet. Music as entertainment excites and indulges us with playfulness and hope. Music when it is used for spiritual practice concentrates and focuses our souls on unseen depths beyond the sway of words.

Music practice, like Centering Prayer, attempts to bring us to a point of deep awareness, a place where thoughts are set aside so that we may rest in the divine presence. In Centering Prayer, a sacred word or mantra is used to signal that our intent in the time of meditation is to be in God's presence. In music practice, it is not a word that we use to call us back to our intent, but a note. When we are engaged in the practice and find our minds wanting to impose their endless cacophony of thoughts on us, we simply return to the notes that linger and roll around us like a refreshing mist on a hot day. We're not trying to listen to the music to feel it as a stimulus. Instead, we are letting the notes be the means for leading us down, down, down into ourselves and God.

A young piano student once asked his teacher why his music didn't flow easily. He told her that he was anxious and stressed as he tried to read the music and create what he read on the piano. The teacher suggested that he imagine being on stage playing before an audience. The young man went away and tried to do as his teacher had suggested. He found that he became even more anxious and uneasy. He felt his shoulders and neck tightening and beads of perspiration breaking out on his face every time he tried to play. Even though he was practicing all by himself, he kept thinking about people watching him, he kept thinking about their critique, about his inadequacy as an accomplished musician. All these thoughts intensified his stressful experience.

He returned to the teacher and explained what had happened. "My playing has only become more difficult," he said. "Your suggestion has not helped at all. What else can I do?"

The teacher asked him to switch seats for a few minutes. The young man sat down and watched his teacher as she positioned her fingers over the keys. "As I play," she said, "close your eyes and feel the notes' impression on your mind, your body, your soul. Think about nothing but the notes as they swirl and waft around you."

The student tried to do as he was asked. At first, he fidgeted and couldn't stop thinking long enough to pay attention to the notes. Then, without even knowing it, he heard something, felt something deep inside. He no longer knew it was his teacher playing, nor did he care. He no longer noticed his agitation. He had become one with the notes and the notes had become one with him.

When we begin music practice, we are initially surprised by the ease with which we engage it. Perhaps, because music is the second language of the soul, the practice feels native and natural to us. We are not trying so hard to succeed at something that seems unfamiliar. Instead, we find ourselves "powering down." It is as if we have returned to an earlier place where we were not so separate from God. There in the reverberations of the notes on our souls, we feel spiritually agile and at home.

If you are a musician or enjoy listening to music you will be intrigued by the possibilities of music as spiritual practice. Having already experienced the joy of music, you will find it interesting to think about making something so pleasurable into a spiritual practice. If you are more naturally contemplative, music practice will offer another way to access your contemplative side. If you are more active or find it hard to sit through a two-hour symphony performance you may chafe at yet another meditative technique that requires solitude and stillness. The element of grace to be found in music practice, however, will overcome even the heartiest objections. The profound simplicity of music practice and the natural way that it opens us to unknown or unacknowledged rooms of our souls will be enough to make us return to it again and again.

Art

Art is not a handicraft; it is the transmission
of feeling the artist has experienced.
—Leo Tolstoy

Are there any of us who has not stood before a great work of art and felt our hearts drop to our stomachs? Such a moment is a moment of revelation, a moment of awe, a moment of absolute stupefaction in the mystery of our ability to capture the depth and scope of human emotion. We are aware, in that moment, of what is beyond us. We are mute in the face of it. And, though the moment is just that—a moment—we know we have somehow touched the fingertip of God.

Art, whether we are viewers or creators, has the ability to move our souls because it draws on images born from the inner womb of silence. These images that may be primordial or a part of the collective unconscious have the power to lead us to a place where words are unimportant, and only image matters. The image itself is the word. It speaks its own story in silence. It calls up deep feelings in us that may have been denied or avoided or overlooked for some time. As those feelings begin to surface, we are able to encounter and interact with them free of judgment or defense precisely because they are invitatory not accusatory. Hidden in the images is the truth of the artist, the truth of us, the truth of human life, the truth of God. In art practice that truth is not pushed down our throat against our will. Rather, it sweeps across us as real as the wind across a North Dakota plain and we have only to stand in its midst to know its reality.

When we do art practice we enter this reality of God and ourselves on a regular and consistent basis. It requires a willingness to be confronted with images that may leave us feeling uncomfortable or questioning, uncertain or incomplete. Art has a way of creating chaos within us because images are often so much more potent than words. To engage in art practice is to place ourselves in a space that is filled with interior vulnerability. The practice is not about going to an art museum. Nor is it the experience of creating a beautiful product to show to our friends. It is about letting the art itself—viewed or created—lead us to a deeper place of union with God. That will always involve some level of chaos, some level of vulnerability, some level of trust.

For a viewer, art practice involves those first moments of connection. As we sit before the piece of art, whether it be a small icon we hold in our hands, or a huge Rothko at the Museum of Modern Art, we begin to find thoughts, questions, and insights rising in us. We might notice, in a portrait for example, that the model is obviously from a poor or underprivileged class, and yet is wearing a velvet cape. We might wonder about that cape. Where did it come from? Was there wealth that was hidden? Was the cape the one possession that could hide poverty? Then, as we sit longer, the questions take a slight change of tone. What are my velvet capes? Why am I wearing them? Where is my soul in poverty and how am I trying to hide my own emptiness? Then, as we sit yet longer, the questions take another slight detour, all the while drawing us deeper into ourselves and God. What capes have you given me, O God? When do I wear them? How am I poor in soul? Where am I trying to hide my poverty from others? Where am I trying to hide myself from you?

Art practice for a creator asks the questions at a different place and in a different order. We pull out our tools for art making: paint, brushes and canvas, or poster board and stickers, or fabrics and glue, or clay and water. After we have assembled our materials, we begin our practice by being silent and still. When we feel we have entered that space of deep quiet and creativity, we wait for images to form. We may notice that questions are forming in us as the images are attempting to be born. We may find ourselves asking, What is my soul longing for? What am I avoiding or denying? Where am I lacking something? Where do I have abundance? As we reflect on the state of our interior lives, images begin to form, begging to be placed on canvas or sculpted in clay. Then as we begin to create, we go deeper. More thoughts surface, more images form, more insights are revealed, and we begin to fill in the details on the piece of art. As we add more details, we become more and more aware of our own truth and the truth of God. We don't need to be accomplished artists to engage in art practice as a creator. The images can be stick figures, circles that represent rocks, squares that represent buildings. It's not the quality of the finished piece that is important, but the process of creating it.

If you are image-driven, intuitive, and regularly experience life by accessing your right brain faculties, you will find art practice an astonishing way to define and deepen your union with God. It will be a practice that feels timeless. If you primarily access your left-brain, or feel that the best art you have ever done was sculpting a clay cat in elementary school, you may be hesitant to dip your soul into art practice. However, even if you do not see yourself in any way artistic, you can experience art as a spiritual practice by viewing art done by others. What is important is entering the world of images in order to touch and feel in our souls what wants to run and hide. In the relationship that develops, we are amazed to find that there is a reason we call God "Creator."

Movies

Even if I set out to make a film about a fillet of sole,
it would be about me.

—Federico Fellini

It may be odd to imagine that Hollywood could be linked to spiritual practice. Certainly, most of us would agree that movies have more value than mere entertainment. We know that some movies open us to a greater understanding of ourselves and our human experience. One of our spiritual limitations is that we tacitly agree with the concept that holiness is to be found in all of life, in the midst of our everyday activities, but we often don't act upon this truth. We find the truth to be real enough when we suddenly experience or encounter the Holy in an unexpected way, but trusting the truth enough to make it part of a steady, consistent, and regular pattern of spirituality in everyday practice seems a little harder to do. When we think about movie practice, we are tempted to fall into the same distorted pattern. We affirm the spiritual depth to be found in movies when we are unexpectedly moved spiritually by a particular film. That doesn't, however, necessarily imply that we expect to find the holy in every movie we see.

The power of movies in our spiritual lives depends on the way we approach them. We understand deep things best through story and movies provide us with a story. Even more, they provide us with images to go along with the story. We approach a movie with a kind of anticipation and excitement that we don't bring to many other activities of life. We are open, ready to receive, ready to enter into the story with our whole selves. Who has not gone to a movie and been so completely engrossed in the story that it seemed almost a rude return to reality when the lights came on?

Unlike nearly any other activity, movies invite us to enter entirely into them for the full length of the film, and we do. In this, movies are an experience of mindfulness. We are attentive, aware, involved, engaged, and without distraction for a significant period of time. While we're in the midst of a movie, we aren't so disturbed by the thoughts of a meeting we have to attend the next day, or what we need to remember to pick up from the grocery store, or what our medical test report will reveal. In fact, we often go to movies precisely so we won't think about all the other demands in our lives. We would find it challenging, to be sure, to be that focused on the present moment if we were sitting on a cushion doing Centering Prayer for two hours. We can use movies, then, as a way to strengthen our mindfulness muscles and as a way to encounter a deeper part of ourselves.

One of the reasons we are able to exercise such focus in a movie is because both hemispheres of our brains are engaged. The right part of the brain is fed by the images, the emotion, the creativity, and the left part by the story itself. The interplay between the actors, the connections to make in the plot, the logical thinking used to move from one scene to the next, the integration of the story with life are all part of the left brain function. When both hemispheres of our brain are engaged, there's little room left for other distractions. This makes movie practice unique among other spiritual practices. While other practices may engage both brain hemispheres at some point during the practice, they do not engage them at the same time, for the same amount of time, or with the concentrated focus that is possible with movie practice. Not to mention, it is an enjoyable practice!

The question is, "How do movies become spiritual practice rather than just entertainment or grist for reflection?" When we begin movie practice we prepare ourselves spiritually using the Preparatory Prayer Process (see pages 132–134). This orients us toward God, toward the reason for which we are practicing— deepening our union with the Holy One. As with other practices, movie practice needs to be consistent. In other words, we don't just choose movies we've been waiting to see, or that we think will be good. We don't just go when it is convenient or we're in the mood. We go regularly, consistently, even if we are not terribly interested in the movie that is playing. In truth, we can meet God in any story—we just have to be open to the movement of God's spirit of truth and insight wherever and however it is manifested.

As we watch the movie, we watch the movie. We let the movie do what it does—engage us completely. The work of spiritual insight will come later. In the immediate moments following the movie's end, we pay attention to the feelings and emotions that dash across our souls like a herd of galloping horses. Holding these in mind will be important when we begin the final stage of the practice, when we are in a quiet place and able to ask ourselves three questions: Where was the image and presence of God in this movie? What emotions in me are a reaction or response to that divine presence? Where do I hear God's Spirit trying to say something to my soul?

It doesn't matter if the movie is a good one or a bad one; these questions can still be considered and answered. It doesn't matter if the movie is spiritual in tone or not, these questions can still be considered and answered. It is the story, the images, and the presence of God in the midst of it all, which makes it possible to take the loose and even tattered threads of the movie and weave them into a fresh pattern of meaning for our souls.

Most of us, no matter what our spiritual personality might be, will find movie practice attractive simply because it is such a complete practice in terms of the engagement of the mind and the emotions. What will become challenging about the practice is the regularity it requires and the deep inner reflection that is a crucial part of the practice. Yet, if you embrace it, you will find that the creative spirit of Hollywood is simply another face of the Spirit of God. Where our hearts and souls are open, there we will find God.

Mind
Practice

Reading, Study, Writing, Consciousness

Reading

*A good book is the precious life-blood of the master spirit,
embalmed and treasured up on purpose for a life beyond.*
—John Milton

Words have power because they communicate the whole of
human life either silently or aloud. They communicate fact and
falsehood. They communicate emotion and feeling, questions and
uncertainty, hopefulness and despair. Words are one of the means
we use for sense-making. Much of what we learn about our world
and about ourselves comes from words.

Sometimes when words can't be spoken, their power is intensified. When Zechariah uttered the words, "His name is John,"
at the naming ceremony for his son, John the Baptist, they were
particularly potent because Zechariah had spent the previous nine
months mute—unable to speak. In the space of silence, words still
conveyed meaning in his mind, and when his speech was restored,
his words were clear, direct, and without pretense. We don't know
what written words Zechariah might have been exposed to during
those nine months, but we know that words still strutted across the
stage of his heart, his mind, and his soul.

Reading is something we do almost without thinking. Because our everyday lives offer us innumerable opportunities to read—everything from email to prayers—we can take the gift of reading for granted, simply because it is such a natural part of our daily lives. We are familiar with spiritual reading—reading holy books that are good for spiritual edification. The tradition of holy reading done in monasteries is a good example of this. During silent meals, one of the monks reads spiritual material to the other monks as they eat so that their souls as well as their bodies are nourished. As in *Lectio Divina*, the passage is read and the listener hears and reflects deeply on the text to understand it more fully and to find ways to apply it to life. Reading as a spiritual practice, however, is not focused necessarily on spiritually oriented books, nor is it only a reflection on what has been read.

The practice involves entering into the words of a story or essay in order to meet and commune with God and find in the interchange a new way of thinking and being for ourselves. John Milton's quote above suggests that couched within the words of a book is a treasure to be discovered—a treasure that holds promise for this life and the life to come. Reading practice turns us into literary archaeologists. We dig and scrape to find the treasure that lies hidden within the words on the page. We lift layers to see what is beneath. Some of what we sort through is dust and dirt that can easily be tossed away. Some of what we uncover has real value for us. We may attempt to determine its origin, or date its impact on our lives, or analyze it to see what intersection it might make in our current experience. Then, as we keep digging, we find some truths that don't seem to make any sense at all. They will need further analysis. And, once in awhile, we hit on something big, something we had never thought we would find, something that makes our heart skip a beat. We find a treasure for our souls that could so easily have been missed had we not persevered in the digging process. We pull out that treasure, dust off the caked mud, and are astonished by what we see.

Reading practice requires this steady commitment to digging. Like a true archaeologist, we bring our souls to it with anticipation and expectation, trusting that we will find something that will surprise us, believing that we may find the very thing for which our souls hunger. It doesn't matter what book we choose to read. What matters is the hope we bring to the reading. If we come to the practice in faith that what we need will be given, we will find that, over time, we will indeed discover truths about ourselves and God that might never have been discovered otherwise.

After we have prepared ourselves for the practice and begin the reading, there are three steps that will help us in the digging process. First, we need to read slowly and in small bites. Archaeologists don't try to excavate an entire site all at once. They focus on a small area at a time until all the ground has been searched and all the relics have been removed. Then the archaeologist moves to another area of the site. In reading practice, there is always more area to cover than we can imagine. As Solomon said, there is no end to the number of books. So we excavate in small areas and dig until there is nothing more to find.

Second, when we read, we read. When we uncover some new truth, we don't need to attempt to gather all of its history and impact in that moment. Like the archaeologist, if we recognize that we have actually found something, we set it aside and keep digging. When we're done for the day, we gather up our finds and take them back to camp for further study and reflection. It may be helpful to simply jot down in a journal what we have found for further reflection later.

Third, we settle ourselves in God's presence and begin to reflect on what we have found. We might ask ourselves such questions as: Why does this seem important? When do I find this operative in my life? How do I interfere with the grace this has to offer? Where is God trying to nudge me? Again, it may be useful to jot down some notes that will help us to internalize and integrate the truths we have found.

If you are more interior and reflective you will gravitate easily to reading practice, finding that it nourishes and tends your soul. If you like to read for entertainment or escape, or prefer action to contemplation, you may find the practice more difficult to embrace. But when the digging produces kernels of insight, nuggets of unexpected truth, and a sure and certain sense of God's presence, even the most resistant will find this a practice worthy of the effort.

GALILEO GALILEI

Study

Study how water flows in a valley stream, smoothly and freely between the rocks. Also learn from holy books and wise people. Everything—even mountains, rivers, plants and trees—should be your teacher.

—Morihei Ueshib

It's all about the way we approach life. Life is always ready to be our teacher, if only we are ready to learn. Most of us look forward to learning new things because God has given us a spirit of curiosity and we enjoy satisfying that curiosity. In fact, if a survey were conducted asking people what they would like to study, the answers would be infinitely different, but everyone would have an answer. We all have something we want to know about. But because life often comes at us with the force of a snowstorm through the Wyoming mountains, we sometimes have to learn on the fly. We ask questions of those who have information we need, or we search the Internet for the resources that we require. We may be able to fit in a yoga class once a week, or an hour-long Bible study, but we don't feel we have the luxury of doing formal study be it in a classroom or along a riverside. Instead, we pick up what we can as we can, gleaning the remnants others have left behind. We are so busy trying to get through the snowstorm that we put off our plans for study to sometime in the future.

Study practice feels like a practice in stability. It helps us plant ourselves firmly even when life seems chaotic. Study asks us to claim our curiosity and go in search of what will nourish it. Study practice is a way to respond to the movement of God's Spirit in us. That movement is an invitation to become more fully human, and to develop more wonder at the vast possibilities that all of life offers. What makes study practice a spiritual practice, and not merely an activity of personal development, is that it inspires our awe at the same time that it deepens our understanding. We do not study only for the sake of gaining knowledge. We filter the learning through the action of God behind the learning.

A young disciple went to the master and asked how he might grow more in the knowledge and love of God. He had read the words in scripture, but could not seem to apply them. He said to the master, "I study my lessons as I am required to do. I try to love God especially in my worship. Still my soul feels empty." The master looked at the disciple with love in his eyes. "Let your study take you into the love of God. Let your worship take you into the love of God. Let your eating take you into the love of God. Let your serving take you into the love of God. When you are taken into the love of God, your study, your worship, your eating, your serving will fill your soul."

One of the reasons for doing spiritual practice at all is to help us connect what occurs in our lives with the reality of God's love in all the activities of life. The dualism that is so prevalent in our culture and in our own lives all too often keeps activity separate from God. Spiritual practice becomes an exercise used to shore up our spiritual sides so we are more able to deal with the physical demands of our lives. If instead, we engage in spiritual practice in order to eliminate the distinctions between spirituality and physical activity, we will find that we whisk away dualism in favor of divine union.

Study practice, more than other practices, helps us clearly see how habituated we are to dualistic living and thinking. Because our minds are so active in study practice, the reality of dualism stands out like red wine poured out on a tablecloth of pure white linen. We see it for what it is—an illusion that keeps our souls from their hunger for union.

As with other practices, we begin study practice with preparation. We center ourselves in the love of God before beginning to do the work of study. It's the intentional placing of ourselves in the love and presence of God that opens our souls to what we will learn and to the spiritual integration of those learnings. After preparation, we bring our whole attention to the endeavor of learning. It doesn't matter if our study is of a foreign language, a new exercise regimen, or research for a class we want to teach; we need to give ourselves permission to set aside other demands and distractions in order to approach our study with the laser-beam penetration we would bring to any meditative practice. Following the completion of our study, we re-affirm our placement in the love and presence of God, and offer prayers of gratitude for the wonders of the mind, the wonders of life, the wonders of spiritual context, and the wonders of the world.

If you are reflective, contemplative, or enjoy the process of serious study, you will find this practice a feast for your soul. If you find it hard to sit still and focus on a single topic, or enjoy working more with people than concepts, you may wonder if study practice will benefit you. It is important to remember, however, that it isn't the particular practice chosen that is crucial. What leads us toward spiritual wholeness is the connection we make between the love of God and the physical activity of everyday life.

Writing

I must write it all out, at any cost. Writing is thinking,
it is more than living, for it is being conscious of living.
—Anne Morrow Lindbergh

There are some things that can come out of us only by writing them down. Writing connects us with our feelings and emotions, with our creativity and fantasies, with our doubts and questions, and with the deepest core of our beings. Consequently, writing is never an easy task. When we speak, we usually deal only with what is front and center of our minds or emotions. We think, we feel, we speak. When we write, we find ourselves going deeper down into what we're thinking and feeling, rather than merely recording what is bubbling at the surface. We begin to see that there are other situations, other encounters, other reactions and responses that have been a part of the current circumstance about which we are writing. Those other strands require not only a benevolent glance, but a studied reflection in order to complete the writing we have begun.

The goal of writing is not necessarily to produce a product— whether we try to write a book or to write as a spiritual practice. The goal of writing is to drop down into the well. It is only when we squarely look at what is hidden in the dark water that we are able to make sense of what we see in the light. This is not to say that the dark water is filled with negative or shameful images. It's that the dark water of the well contains all of our lives. What we've thought and considered, what we've hoped for and dreamt, what we've felt and said, who we've met and loved and why is all a part of that dark water in the well. Our identity, and the integration of our identity with God's image of us, occurs when we grapple with all the wondrous and not so wondrous elements that we find in that dark water. Many of us do this work through psychotherapy or other forms of psychological introspection. Yet, writing is often a part of those therapies precisely because it takes us deep into that inner well.

Anne Morrow Lindbergh, the famous aviator, understood this. As she said, "Writing is...more than living, for it is being conscious of living." From the moment that we begin to scratch a word on a page we are conscious of living. If we are recording how angry we are, we are conscious of the life force of anger. If we are writing about a new idea for church growth, we are conscious of the life force of regeneration. If we are writing about grief, we are conscious of the life force of sadness and death. Some activities in life have become so rote that we do them on auto-pilot. We don't need to think or question. We simply do them. We're like a cow following the herd. We don't think about it. We just do it. Writing never becomes so familiar that we can do it on auto-pilot. It always engages us at a level where we become conscious of life.

Writing as a spiritual practice is not simply about keeping a journal. Journaling is, too often, an exercise we do when we have something to write about. That is, when we have a new thought or insight, or we have a profound understanding of something that we want to capture on the page, or are struck by a memory that begs to be recorded, or we don't want to forget a theme or point that we want to reflect on in the future. While those are all important, they do not constitute writing practice. Writing practice, as in all the other practices, is something we commit to doing regularly and consistently, whether we have something we think we need to write about or not. In fact, writing practice is often the most fruitful when we sit at the blank page and feel that we have absolutely nothing at all to put down on the paper. That is often the time we go deepest into the well, and draw up from its waters the most meaningful spiritual and personal insights. The most important element of writing practice is the commitment to do it whether or not we have anything to write. Writing practice is arguably one of the most difficult of all the practices, because the blank page forces faith. We face the issue of faith every time we engage in this practice.

We prepare ourselves with the Preparatory Prayer Process (see pages 132–134) then take pen in hand and look at the blank page. The act of faith occurs right then and there. Do we trust ourselves enough to believe that we will have the courage to drop into the well to draw up some water of life? Do we trust that when we drop down, God will be there and help us sort through all the debris that comes up in our buckets? There's no hiding, denying, avoiding. The blank page is waiting to be filled and it will take faith to fill it. We simply have to trust that if we are still before the page, something will flow from our pen onto that page. Writing practice takes us down deep where we meet ourselves and God. Then it brings us up and out with new hope and understanding and gives us the potential of becoming more than we ever thought we could be.

It is not impossible to use the computer for writing practice, but the results will not be as fulfilling. The reason for this is that most of us type more quickly than we write. Consequently, we will not go as deep down into the well using the computer because we can get in and out too quickly. Physical writing, because we do it more slowly, takes us deeper for longer. We draw out more, we nuance more, the images and ideas play in our mind more. Writing practice will be most beneficial if it is done with a physical pen and pad of paper.

If you are reflective or enjoy writing you will quickly be attracted to writing practice. The challenge, however, will be writing when you feel you have nothing to write about. If you would rather wrestle with a crocodile than write in a journal, you may be more resistant to the practice. In fact, for everyone, writing practice seems to invite every excuse for avoidance. But if you can break free of your resistance, you will be delightfully surprised to come to a deeper knowledge of yourself and God more quickly than you would ever have thought possible.

Consciousness

*Consciousness succumbs all too easily to unconscious influences,
and these are often truer and wiser than our conscious thinking.*

—Carl Gustav Jung

So much of the mind can remain invisible or hidden over the course of our lives, simply because we don't engage the deeper parts of it with the same attention that we give to the thoughts and ideas that are so near the surface clamoring for attention. Whether it's what we're going to have for dinner, or what subject we want to raise at a meeting, or how to help our child through a troubling period, or even how beautiful the weather is outside, we are more accustomed to giving heed to what nudges and gropes at us like a needy child, than we are to uncovering and discovering what lies in the silent and unseen places of our minds. Even though we may not do the sleuthing work to see what treasures lie there, psychologists will tell us that most of our responses, in thought and behavior, are centered in this mostly untapped unconscious part of our being.

The word consciousness simply means internal knowledge. When our unconscious remains unexplored, we are deprived of that fuller internal knowledge. The more we expose ourselves to our unconscious, the fuller we become as human beings and children of God. Consciousness practice is the intentional and specific commitment to explore this part of our brains. We might say it is the practice of bringing the unconscious forward into the conscious mind. While there are many ways to access our unconscious, from therapy to meditation, consciousness practice here will mean the exercise of using inner dialogue and journaling to coax out the tendrils of our deepest souls. The more we are able to encounter and interact with our unconscious, the better we will understand ourselves, our relationships, and our souls. While consciousness practice makes use of writing as a way to expose ourselves to ourselves, as it were, it is not the same as journaling. The goal is not keeping a record of thoughts, feelings, and insights. The blank page becomes the canvas upon which we tease out what remains unseen and unknown within us. Sometimes this will occur through words, sometimes through images. It involves the process of dialogue or conversation with what is present in our deepest core, but still hidden from view. As that dialogue or conversation finds its way onto the page, a fuller integration between conscious and unconscious begins to occur.

Our lives are replete with experiences, feelings, and memories that have helped shape us into what we are. Some of these are readily available to the conscious mind. We easily recall them, even reminisce about them. Then there are memories that seem less accessible to the conscious brain—things that are too painful, too important, or too powerful to remember in vivid detail. Even though they are not eagerly pressing upon our minds and emotions, they are shaping our lives. When we begin to work with our unconscious through the writing and dialogue process, we become more familiar with those memories and are often surprised by the wisdom they have to share with us. It is important to remember that consciousness practice is not psychotherapy. It is a form of spiritual remembering and reflection, though it may be that dialoging or writing about certain parts of our unconscious will point to a need for a therapist or spiritual director to help us sort through the emotions and memories we encounter. We might avoid this practice because we are uneasy or fearful about delving so deeply into ourselves. Or, we may think that the practice is oriented too heavily on the self, rather than others. Or, we may wonder if God is at work or if we are simply engaging in some form of spiritual navel-gazing. While these are valid concerns, the truth is that, at its core, consciousness practice is really no different than any other form of meditation that leads us more deeply into ourselves and God.

When we begin consciousness practice we center ourselves in the presence of God through silence or some form of quiet prayer or meditative music. We offer ourselves—the parts known and unknown to us—completely to God asking that we might bear witness to the miracle of our own lives that have been given to us by God. Then, we begin the writing process using some sentence or image to "prime the pump," so to speak. We write what we're feeling, and then we become still and allow ourselves to go more deeply within. Then we wait—just as we wait for God's felt presence in centering prayer. Words will begin to form in us, or feelings will be released in us. As we notice the words or feelings, we simply have a conversation with them and write out our conversation as it is taking place, as a way to capture what our unconscious might be trying to say to us. If we don't take the energy to do the writing, there is a distinct possibility that when we have brought the meditation to a close we will have very little recollection of what transpired within us. The writing is a physical and tangible way to keep us focused during the practice, and also provides a written record of what we have experienced. It is this process of writing and later reflecting on what has been written that helps us internalize the wisdom offered to us by our unconscious. Rather than being a reflective writing exercise, consciousness practice places our conversation in the presence of God where we are able to continually ask for a deeper and more enlightened understanding of what we are learning about ourselves.

If you like to write and reflect, and are intrigued at the prospect of peeling away the layers of your inner being, you will find consciousness practice a vital form of self-revelation. You will find it nourishing to notice how the unconscious is directing your conscious mind. If you do not find journaling an easy or helpful exercise, you may immediately turn away from consciousness practice because of the journaling component. As you experiment with the practice, however, you may find that journaling need not be full sentences and paragraphs. Rather, the journal is the recording tool for what you learn. Any word or phrase that accurately records what is occurring is sufficient. More importantly, when the unconscious begins to surface and you learn how to make use of the lessons the unconscious offers, gratitude for the practice and for the wisdom of God will overcome any initial hesitation that you experienced in the beginning. In truth, God is present in both our unconscious and our conscious. Our task is to find God in both.

Movement Practice

Body Movement, Walking, Nature, Handwork

Body Movement

The dancer of the future will be one whose body and soul have grown so harmoniously together that the natural language of that soul will have become the movement of the body.

—Isadora Duncan

Exercise, in and of itself, is not spiritual practice. It is exercise. It is a way to strengthen and tone the body, improve the heart rate, increase the circulation, and burn excess calories in order to stay healthy. Yet, exercise can become spiritual practice when we attentively and intentionally bring the soul into the movement. St. Paul said that the training of the body brings limited benefit, but the training of the soul is valuable in every way because it holds promise not only for this life but for the life to come (I Timothy 4:8). When we bring body and soul together in movement, we increase the value of each.

Some body movement routines are naturally suited to soul practice. Yoga and Tai Chi, for example, are meditative and reflective exercises that can give us the space and opportunity to pray with our breath, to pray with slow movement, to pray with the stretch and release of our muscles. The Sanskrit word "yoga" literally means "yoking or union with the Supreme Spirit."

Yoga uses postures, breath, and meditation to join the body with the Divine Spirit. Tai Chi, though formally a martial art, uses slow, smooth, and graceful body movements to bring the mind and body into a state of relaxation. With each successive movement in the routine, the body and muscles relax more. With the release of stress and the increase of calm, we find that prayer and meditation are no longer just spiritual demands—we find they actually take us deeper into our bodies and deeper into God.

Other forms of exercise that are not as reflective as yoga or tai chi can still become spiritual practice for us. Some ideas might include: engaging in intercessory prayer while we swim laps, praying a mantra while we jog, whispering the Jesus Prayer while we work with free weights, or praying Morning Prayer through our iPods while we bicycle. What makes any exercise a spiritual practice is how we intentionally bring our souls into the movement of our body.

When we begin to use body movement as spiritual practice three things begin to happen. First, we become aware of the intense connection between body and soul, between earth and heaven, between creature and Creator. We realize the impact each has on the other. This is easily missed in the hustle and bustle of everyday life. But, when the body is healthy, the soul more easily communes with God. When the soul is healthy, the body more easily communes with God. When we engage in body movement practice, the interrelation between the two becomes undeniable.

Second, we stop seeing exercise as an end in itself. If we enjoy the experience of exercise, we may engage in it because we want to accrue the benefits it has to offer. If we dislike the experience of exercise, we may avoid it with fortitude we don't expend anywhere else in our lives. We may be aware of its benefits, but have no motivation to perspire in order to enjoy them. When, however, we do exercise as spiritual practice—when it involves both body and soul—we find ourselves beginning to desire fullness and strength in our souls, yes—but also in our bodies.

Finally, we begin to hear the voice of God through our bodies as well as our souls. We become attuned to the subtle advances God makes toward us. We feel our bodies straining to hear God more fully and see God more clearly. At the same time, we feel our souls seeking the filling of God through the very movements that we use as we exercise our muscles and joints. Sometimes we find that what we could not hear clearly in silent meditation becomes crystal clear in the middle of a particular movement.

If you are active, you will be attracted to body movement practice. For you, the combination of body and soul can occur more powerfully than it would be were you to sit motionless on a meditation pad for hours on end. If your meditation pad is your closest companion you may, at first, find it difficult to get out of a sitting or kneeling posture in order to put the body into motion while praying with the soul. You may not think it is even possible to meld the two. Yet, the power of body movement is so strong, that it won't take more than two or three sessions with the practice to be convinced of the efficacy of movement to show that body and soul have grown so harmoniously together that the natural language of that soul has become the movement of the body.

Walking

It is not talking but walking that will bring us to heaven.
—Matthew Henry

There is an interesting connection between bread baking and walking. Anyone who bakes bread knows that there are at least two important aspects of baking a delicious loaf—the temperature of the yeast and the quality of the kneading. Both the yeast and the kneading help make the dough full. Strong and deep kneading rolls the dough around and presses it down again, over and over, until bubbles are eliminated. If kneading is shortened or weak, those bubbles will end up as empty holes in the finished loaf. The Old Middle Dutch word for walking, *walken*, means to knead or press full. Like kneading bread, walking has the capacity to knead our souls until they are full.

Naturalists, like Thoreau, have touted the value of walking to strengthen the body, mind, and soul. Contemporary exercise gurus have, likewise, convinced us of the importance of walking as a way to exercise every muscle in the body. This exercise is a kind of kneading—twisting, rolling, turning, and pressing down—that not only relaxes the body, but also tightens it. It removes the bubbles that leave the body loose and unfit, just as it removes the bubbles that leave the soul loose and unfit.

The spiritual practice of walking has been an important part of Eastern religions for centuries. Meditative walking is as much a part of spiritual practice as sitting meditation. In many Buddhist communities, for example, sitting meditation is followed by walking meditation, which leads back to sitting meditation and the process continues again. Meditative walking involves mindful attention to each step taken, to the in-breath and the out-breath. Meditative walking is usually done slowly with no particular destination in mind. It is walking in order to walk. It is the reason for the practice and the end of the practice. The time spent in the middle is time of union with the Divine. It is not only a way to move the body, it is also a way to engage in the same pattern of meditation experienced while sitting in silence on a meditation cushion.

In recent years in the West, meditative walking a labyrinth has become a part of many people's spiritual practice. Labyrinths provide a confined area in which to walk mindfully. Since there are no ends on a labyrinth, there is no fear of getting lost. Once we start on the path and put one foot in front of the other, we will end up in the center and come back out again at our starting place. The simple pattern of a labyrinth is actually geometrically formed from a cross, and labyrinths in the Middle Ages were used in churches and cathedrals as a way for new Christians to make a symbolic pilgrimage to Jerusalem. Like any pilgrimage, the labyrinth provides time for reflection, time for prayer, time to pay attention, time to breathe, time to have our souls kneaded by the hand of God.

Meditative walking, however, is not limited to labyrinth walking. You can do it in your living room, in a parking lot, down a country lane, or through a bustling city. What it requires is not a particular place, but a settling of the soul into the activity. It is a practice of mindfulness that trains the soul to rest in the presence of God amidst activity. In this, it is not exercise for exercise's sake. Walking practice is active, but is meant to slow us down. It is not a power walk supplemented with prayer, but an intentional and focused pattern of movement meditation.

When we begin walking practice, we may notice that we tend to walk too fast, we try too hard to get somewhere, we hurry to complete the journey. Or, we may find ourselves turning into quasi-naturalists—focusing on the landscape or people around us to help alleviate our boredom. Or we may wonder what the point is, what we're really supposed to be doing, what we should expect to receive from our effort. And, like any other form of meditation or contemplative prayer, we may find ourselves thinking, planning, or strategizing. For this reason, it's good to have a short prayer or phrase to say that can help us align our steps and our breath to help focus your heart on union with God. Then, when we find ourselves thinking or planning or scheming, we are able to simply return to the prayer, to the step, to the breath, to God.

Walking practice will slow us down and open us up. It will tighten the empty pockets in our souls and make us full. We will find ourselves weary from using muscles we had not used before, and energized by the same use of those muscles. We will begin to see the importance of movement as a way to meditate, and that same meditation will begin to spill out into all the movements of our lives.

If you like to walk, this practice will be attractive to you. But it may be particularly challenging to walk without purpose or destination. To walk only to walk in the presence of God. To walk in order to knead your soul, rather than your body, into shape. If you find it challenging to be attentive during sitting meditation you may, at first, be reluctant to try walking practice, thinking that walking will be over-stimulating and keep you from the spiritual focus you need. What is surprising, however, is that walking practice actually leads us more deeply inward than we would have thought possible. Rather than over-stimulating us, we find that we become more internally quiet and still. Even when we are surrounded by sights and sounds we find stillness. In that stillness, the hand of heaven kneads our souls into shape and we are strangely pressed full with God.

Nature

All these things remind me that nature is as much a mirror of God's word and wisdom as any words of ours can be.

—Perrin Radley

Most of us have been awed, amazed, astonished by the wonder of the world. If there is anything that confirms to us the reality and presence of God, it is the order and mystery of creation. We can see a freshly opened flower, a newborn puppy, a stunning sunrise, or a laboring ant, and find ourselves breathless. Even though we have explored and investigated nature to better understand it, we can never exhaust its endless supply of miracles. In fact, many of us believe in miracles because we first witnessed them in creation.

The more we know about nature, the more we realize that it is our responsibility to protect it. The emphasis on caring for the earth as God's own creation, the urgency to halt overconsumption, the attention needed to reverse global warming, the emergence of eco-tours in lieu of vacations, all point to the priority we know needs to be placed on the health of the planet in order to preserve, protect, and replenish it. It is easy to have concern for the earth, and even work to be better stewards of its resources and yet fail to see the power it has to draw us more deeply into the embrace of heaven. Nature as a spiritual practice takes us from the point of seeing God's presence in the world around us, to actually allowing that world to be the medium through which we develop union with the Divine.

The word nature comes from the Latin word natus, which means to be born. As Christians, we are familiar with the phrase, "*deus incarnatus est*"—*God is born in flesh.* God is born into nature. Recognizing and affirming this truth is a critical aspect of nature practice, as is the recognition and affirmation that we have been born into nature. When we recognize and affirm both of these things, we come to understand also that nature is the ground upon which the two are joined—human and divine, earth and heaven, material and immaterial, corruptible and incorruptible, finite and infinite. It is here—in the reality of soil and leaf, rodents and big cats, water and fire, storm and earthquake, petals and stalks—that we have the opportunity to become one with God, to have our heart knit to God, as the Psalmist says (Psalm 86:11).

Nature practice is more than simply appreciating and being grateful for the beauties of creation. It is finding the path for divine union within the vehicle of nature. There are several ways that this can happen. If we're more contemplative, we can place ourselves in nature and wait in silence and stillness for the presence of God to be felt and known. When we are distracted by thoughts or ideas, we simply return, not to a mantra or sacred word, but to the reality of the nature around us. In this sense, the natural area in which we find ourselves becomes the mantra or the sacred word. If we are more active, we can use nature itself as a way to communicate with God. After being attentively present to the nature area, we can open our hearts to vocal prayer or the recitation of psalms. We may even be moved to write our own psalms and prayers. If we are inclined to draw or paint, nature can become the brush through which we paint our hearts for God. After affirming God's presence in the nature area, we might turn our eyes inward and see how God brings that space alive in the depth of our creative spirit. Our response to God might be a work of art, a poem, a song, a story.

Nature practice has the capacity not only to bring our souls into deeper union with God, but to give them life. When our souls feel flat or lackluster, when we feel that we're walking on a spiritual treadmill, when other spiritual practices seem to leave us eager for more, nature practice—*natus* practice—allows new life to be born in us.

Every spiritual personality is attracted to this practice because there are so many different ways to engage in it. Perhaps because God was born into nature, as were all of us, no one finds nature practice an empty or vacuous way to encounter the Holy. Somehow in our own birth and the birth of the Word, there is the invitation to bond with life that is so fresh and real in the smallest speck of dust or the greatest depth of ocean.

Elizabeth Browning penned the famous and familiar words, "Earth is crammed with heaven. /Every bush is aflame with the fire of God,/but only those who see take off their shoes." This is the truth of nature practice—a truth that becomes ever-present and real when we consistently bring ourselves into that space where nature can reveal to us the whisper and grace of God. Often, we are so powerfully aware of that whisper and grace that we take off the shoes of our souls with the enthusiasm of a child ready to dig their feet into the wet sand at the beach. There is, however, a final phrase to Browning's words that is less familiar to us: "*The rest just pick the berries.*" We do a lot of berry picking of the earth, and are surprised when both the earth and our souls suffer. Nature practice helps us take off our shoes rather than merely pick berries.

Handwork

Sewing mends the soul. . . .
—Author unknown

One of the reasons we find spiritual practice difficult to maintain is because, too often, the quality of our results is sporadic. When we begin practice we expect to have an experience of communion with God and sometimes we do achieve that communion. But at other times it feels as if we have simply put in time and have garnered no useful result. During the times when we are keenly aware of God's presence, we are spurred onward for the next session of practice. We want to duplicate what we have so recently experienced. Conversely, when God seems as silent as the dead tree or as distant as the moon, we may find it difficult to continue the practice. In short, we know we are spiritually hungry, but we are also spiritual perfectionists who have become spiritually greedy. If we can't get what we need or want, we're disheartened. If our practice time is unfulfilling in some way, we feel either we, or God, have failed.

What we benefit from most in spiritual practice, however, is not what is received at a discrete individual session. Rather, it is the steady, consistent, repetitive actions taken over time that carve the soul into a purer image of the Divine.

Repetition, the great winnower of sharp edges, is an ally to the soul's development. Paradoxically when repetition seems boring or lackluster, we find its very sameness drops us down into depths never charted by those insistent on novelty. If we really seek to know God, if we truly desire to grow more and more into the image and likeness of Christ, if we long for our souls to be grounded in the reality of heaven, then repetition is a path for arriving there.

It may not be readily apparent how handwork practice can be a vehicle for this depth of knowing God. After all, what can knitting or weaving have to do with the Holy? How can threading a needle and pulling it in and out of fabric strengthen the soul? As it is, if we are not needle workers, we can find ourselves slightly irritated at those who knit or work needlepoint during a meeting. The concept of finding God in the process of doing handwork may seem a little farfetched.

Consider, for a moment, the practice of praying with beads. The two elements most important in that practice are that our hands and our minds are kept busy so that we can meditate more deeply. When contemplative prayer leaves us feeling like the thought police, when our prayer period is as jumpy as a grasshopper, we might try handwork practice. Once we learn a particular handwork practice, we just need to do the repetitive, reflective work and we'll be surprised at the height at which our soul ascends or the depth with which it descends into the heart of God.

If we are already accustomed to doing handwork or know the basic skills of handwork, turning it into spiritual practice requires only a slight shift in the mind and heart. If we lack skills in handwork, we may need to give time to learning before we begin the actual practice. Otherwise, we will find ourselves focused on the mechanics, rather than on the meditation. When we engage in handwork practice, we are not really all that interested in the product. Instead we are interested in keeping our minds and hands engaged so that we are able to fully attend to God. So, our skill level need not be perfect, but we do need to know enough of the basics, that we can do them without thinking or reading directions or figuring out where our fingers go next. Whatever type of handwork we choose to use for the practice, all we need to do is learn enough to do the basics without thinking. If, for example, we learn how to do a knitting stitch and simply knit, row after row, we will find our soul quieting, then expanding, then deepening. It won't matter that we aren't creating a fabulous sweater. What will matter is the steady clicking of the needles, the regular movements of our hands with the yarn, the repetitive beginning and ending of row after row.

As we settle into the rhythm of the handwork, we will also find ourselves settling into the rhythm of communion with God. We will find ourselves judging our consistency and our perfectionism less in this practice. Instead, we will simply sit with God as we do our handwork. When we find ourselves wandering away from God in our mind, we simply return to the stitches. We might say a prayer of return, or a prayer for continued presence, or a prayer for openness. In any case, silently and stealthily, God will be molding and shaping our soul as our hands move and our minds calm.

If you are good with your hands or already do handwork for relaxation or to strengthen clarity of mind, you will naturally want to embrace handwork as a spiritual practice. Your challenge will be to step away from the inclination to create a product so that the action of the handwork becomes the tool that quiets your soul enough for deep attention to God. If you feel inept with such things as handwork, or can't imagine taking the time to learn a handwork skill, you might dismiss the practice as irrelevant. It might be, however, the very thing that will restore a sense of curiosity and challenge to a practice that has become stale or lifeless. It's not each session of practice that determines the state of our souls, but the whole of practice that transforms our lives.

A Process for Beginning a Spiritual Practice

Preparation is a necessary part of spiritual practice. Sometimes, we may feel like jumping in without preparation, but preparation is important for three reasons. First, it helps us make an internal shift from the thought patterns and activities that have engaged us. In other words, it helps us make the transition from what we've been doing to what we are going to do. Second, it gives us a way of naming an intention for the practice. That is, we offer to God what we hope to bring of ourselves to the practice. Finally, it helps us place our souls into a waiting and receptive state. This helps us acknowledge that we are in God's presence and affirms that we are open to that presence. The preparation phase of spiritual practice need not be long or arduous, but it does need to be intentional. This is not to say that God is not always present with us, or that we are not always ready to pray. If, however, we take a few moments to center ourselves on what it is we are about to do, we will find that our souls are more ready to be shaped by what will occur during the time of prayer.

The following preparation process is a general and simple way to ready ourselves for practice. It may need to be modified or adapted to fit a particular practice, but the pattern lends itself to such personal adaptation. There are only four short steps, and each step may be lengthened or shortened as needed.

Quiet yourself

This is more than a state of mind. It is a change in posture—from standing to sitting, or sitting to kneeling, for example. It is a physical way to mark the change from one activity to another. If you were going out jogging, it would be the act of getting up off the couch, putting on your running shoes, and going out the door.

Breathe attentively

To help your body settle into the mindset of practice, it is good to breathe deeply, or to count your breaths for a few moments. As your breathing slows, your heart rate will slow. In that quieted state, the soul gently opens to the presence of God.

Pray

This is a time to center yourself in God's presence. Sometimes the prayer may be extemporaneous. Sometimes it may be a familiar mantra such as The Jesus Prayer. Sometimes it may be a chant or a piece of music. Sometimes it may be the Lord's Prayer or a verse of a hymn that is recited. Sometimes it may be nothing more than a silent acknowledgment of being in God's presence.

Make an Intention

This is an opportunity to give yourself, your time, and your presence to God and offer to God your intention for the time that you will be engaged in the practice. This helps focus the practice and is a touchstone for you to return to throughout the practice.

At the end of the practice, it is helpful to reverse the process with a few changes. Just as there needs to be an internal shift when beginning practice, there needs to be another internal shift as you transition back into the regular round of responsibilities and activities of your day. Again, a simple process will suffice.

Offer gratitude to God

Spend a few moments thanking God for the time that you have spent together and for the lessons or insights that you have received. This may take the form of a prayer, or a smile, or the singing of a hymn. It is a way to let God know that you don't take the time for granted.

Breathe attentively

As you did at the beginning of the practice, breathe deeply or count your breaths for some time. This is a way of becoming aware again of your own body, the noises and sounds around you, the internal movement back into daily activity.

Gather together a nosegay

St. Francis de Sales suggests that a nosegay be taken away from periods of prayer so that when difficulty or stress arise during the day, you can take the nosegay out and inhale its scent. In other words, gather up a few simple thoughts that you want to carry away from the practice. Return to them throughout the day to keep you focused on God.

Create a record

If you like to journal and have the time to do it, it is a good idea to write down what occurred during the practice—your feelings, your hopes, the intention you offered, the points of struggle, the insights or learnings. Even if writing is not something you are naturally drawn to, it is good to jot down in a small notebook two or three notes or phrases about the time spent in prayer. This becomes a spiritual log, of sorts. It helps you see, over time, the tenderness of God, the struggles of your soul, the questions and hopes that are lodged within you, and the grace that is always coming to you from the heart of heaven.